#1 TEACHER

# · FOR THE BEST ·

# TEACHER

## EVER

summersdale

FOR THE BEST TEACHER EVER

An Hachette UK Company
www.hachette.co.uk

Summersdale Publishers Ltd
Part of Octopus Publishing Group Limited
Carmelite House
50 Victoria Embankment
LONDON
EC4Y 0DZ

www.summersdale.com

Printed and bound in China

ISBN: 978-1-78685-963-1

TO.......................

FROM .................

THE ART OF
TEACHING IS THE
ART OF ASSISTING
DISCOVERY.

Mark Van Doren

THE BEST TEACHERS
TEACH FROM THE
HEART, NOT FROM
THE BOOK.

Anonymous

# I BELIEVE EFFECTIVE LEADERS ARE, FIRST AND FOREMOST, GOOD TEACHERS.

JOHN WOODEN

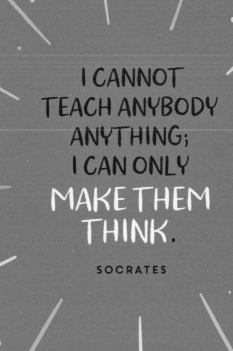

I CANNOT
TEACH ANYBODY
ANYTHING;
I CAN ONLY
MAKE THEM
THINK.

SOCRATES

BEFORE ANY GREAT THINGS
ARE ACCOMPLISHED, A
MEMORABLE CHANGE MUST
BE MADE IN THE SYSTEM
OF EDUCATION... TO
RAISE THE LOWER RANKS
OF SOCIETY NEARER
TO THE HIGHER.

John Adams

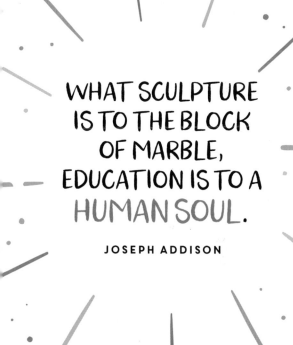

WHAT SCULPTURE
IS TO THE BLOCK
OF MARBLE,
EDUCATION IS TO A
HUMAN SOUL.

JOSEPH ADDISON

IF YOU ARE PLANNING
FOR A YEAR, SOW RICE;
IF YOU ARE PLANNING FOR
A DECADE, PLANT TREES;
IF YOU ARE PLANNING FOR
A LIFETIME, EDUCATE PEOPLE.

Chinese proverb

**"**

THE REAL OBJECT
OF EDUCATION IS
TO GIVE CHILDREN
RESOURCES THAT
WILL ENDURE AS
LONG AS LIFE
ENDURES.

Sydney Smith

THANK

YOU FOR
EVERYTHING

WHEN YOU WANT
TO BUILD A SHIP,
DO NOT BEGIN BY
GATHERING WOOD,
CUTTING BOARDS
AND DISTRIBUTING
WORK, BUT RATHER
AWAKEN WITHIN
MEN THE DESIRE
FOR THE VAST AND
ENDLESS SEA.

ANTOINE DE SAINT-EXUPÉRY

EVERY CHILD DESERVES
A CHAMPION — AN ADULT
WHO WILL NEVER GIVE UP ON
THEM, WHO UNDERSTANDS THE
POWER OF CONNECTION AND
INSISTS THAT THEY BECOME
THE BEST THAT THEY
CAN POSSIBLY BE.

**RITA PIERSON**

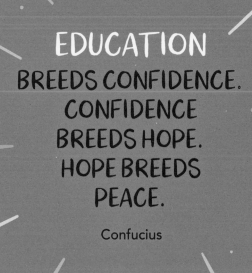

**EDUCATION**
BREEDS CONFIDENCE.
CONFIDENCE
BREEDS HOPE.
HOPE BREEDS
PEACE.

Confucius

IF SOMEONE IS GOING
DOWN THE WRONG ROAD,
HE DOESN'T NEED MOTIVATION
TO SPEED HIM UP. WHAT
HE NEEDS IS EDUCATION
TO TURN HIM AROUND.

**Jim Rohn**

"

TELL ME AND I
FORGET; TEACH ME
AND I REMEMBER;
INVOLVE ME
AND I LEARN.

Benjamin Franklin

"

# THE OBJECT OF TEACHING A CHILD IS TO ENABLE HIM TO GET ALONG WITHOUT HIS TEACHER.

ELBERT HUBBARD

EDUCATION IS NOT
PREPARATION FOR LIFE;
EDUCATION IS LIFE ITSELF.

John Dewey

MAN'S MIND,
ONCE STRETCHED
BY A NEW IDEA,
NEVER REGAINS
ITS ORIGINAL
DIMENSIONS.

OLIVER WENDELL HOLMES JR

**"**

THE FUTURE CANNOT
BE PREDICTED, BUT
FUTURES CAN BE
INVENTED.

Dennis Gabor

**"**

# THE FUNCTION OF EDUCATION... IS TO TEACH ONE TO THINK INTENSIVELY AND TO THINK CRITICALLY.

MARTIN LUTHER KING JR

THE SECRET OF TEACHING IS
TO APPEAR TO HAVE KNOWN
ALL YOUR LIFE WHAT YOU JUST
LEARNED THIS MORNING.

Anonymous

**THANK YOU**

**FOR PUSHING**

**ME TO BE THE**

**BEST I CAN BE**

CHILDREN MUST BE
TAUGHT HOW TO THINK,
NOT WHAT TO THINK.

Margaret Mead

THE PRINCIPAL GOAL OF
EDUCATION IN THE SCHOOLS
SHOULD BE CREATING MEN
AND WOMEN WHO ARE CAPABLE
OF DOING NEW THINGS.

**Jean Piaget**

## A TEACHER IS A COMPASS THAT ACTIVATES THE MAGNETS OF CURIOSITY, KNOWLEDGE AND WISDOM IN THE PUPILS.

Ever Garrison

# WE OFTEN TAKE FOR GRANTED THE VERY THINGS THAT MOST DESERVE OUR GRATITUDE.

CYNTHIA OZICK

# IDEAL TEACHERS

ARE THOSE WHO
USE THEMSELVES
AS BRIDGES OVER
WHICH THEY INVITE
THEIR STUDENTS
TO CROSS.

NIKOS KAZANTZAKIS

EDUCATION IS WHAT
SURVIVES WHEN WHAT
HAS BEEN LEARNED HAS
BEEN FORGOTTEN.

B. F. Skinner

SHALL I TELL YOU
THE SECRET OF THE
TRUE SCHOLAR?
IT IS THIS: EVERY
MAN I MEET IS MY
MASTER IN SOME
POINT, AND IN THAT
I LEARN OF HIM.

**RALPH WALDO EMERSON**

# WHEN YOU LEARN, TEACH.
# WHEN YOU GET, GIVE.

Maya Angelou

A TRULY SPECIAL
TEACHER IS VERY
WISE, AND SEES
TOMORROW
IN EVERY
CHILD'S EYES.

Anonymous

# I AM NOT A TEACHER, BUT AN AWAKENER.

ROBERT FROST

# A CHILD MISEDUCATED
# IS A CHILD LOST.

John F. Kennedy

STUDY AS IF YOU
WERE TO LIVE
FOREVER.

Mahatma Gandhi

**YOU**

**ARE AN**

**INSPIRATION**

WHAT WE LEARN
WITH PLEASURE,
WE NEVER FORGET.

Alfred Mercier

# GOOD TEACHING

IS ONE-FOURTH
PREPARATION AND
THREE-FOURTHS
THEATRE.

GAIL GODWIN

THE MIND IS NOT A VESSEL THAT NEEDS FILLING, BUT WOOD THAT NEEDS IGNITING.

Plutarch

# TEACHERS TOUCH THE FUTURE.

ANONYMOUS

THE BEAUTIFUL THING ABOUT LEARNING IS THAT NO ONE CAN TAKE IT AWAY FROM YOU.

B. B. KING

" BETTER THAN A THOUSAND DAYS OF DILIGENT STUDY IS ONE DAY WITH A GREAT TEACHER.

Japanese proverb

# LOGIC WILL GET YOU FROM A TO B. IMAGINATION WILL TAKE YOU EVERYWHERE.

ALBERT EINSTEIN

EDUCATION IS THE MOST
POWERFUL WEAPON WHICH
YOU CAN USE TO CHANGE
THE WORLD.

Nelson Mandela

TO TEACH IS TO
LEARN TWICE OVER.

Joseph Joubert

THE HARDEST
THING TO TEACH IS
HOW TO CARE.

ANONYMOUS

A TEACHER AFFECTS
ETERNITY; HE CAN
NEVER TELL WHERE
HIS INFLUENCE STOPS.

Henry Adams

**LAUGHTER IS TIMELESS, IMAGINATION HAS NO AGE AND DREAMS ARE FOREVER.**

Anonymous

# EACH OF US HAS A FIRE IN OUR HEARTS FOR SOMETHING. IT'S OUR GOAL IN LIFE TO FIND IT AND KEEP IT LIT.

MARY LOU RETTON

**YOU MAKE**

**LEARNING**

**FUN!**

# EVERY TRUTH

HAS FOUR CORNERS:
AS A TEACHER I
GIVE YOU ONE
CORNER, AND IT IS
FOR YOU TO FIND
THE OTHER THREE.

CONFUCIUS

# THE HIGHEST RESULT OF EDUCATION IS TOLERANCE.

Helen Keller

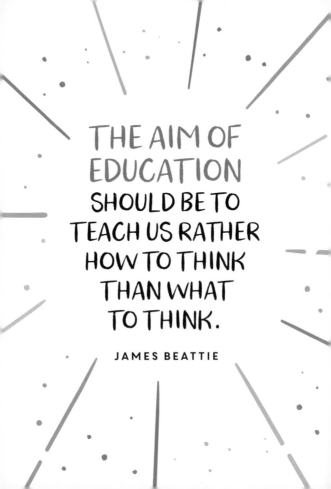

YOU CAN TEACH A
STUDENT A LESSON FOR A
DAY; BUT IF YOU CAN TEACH
HIM TO LEARN BY CREATING
CURIOSITY, HE WILL
CONTINUE THE LEARNING
PROCESS AS LONG
AS HE LIVES.

Clay P. Bedford

**"**

DO NOT CONFINE
YOUR CHILDREN
TO YOUR OWN
LEARNING, FOR
THEY WERE BORN
IN ANOTHER TIME.

Hebrew proverb

**"**

WHO DARES TO TEACH
MUST NEVER CEASE
TO LEARN.

John Cotton Dana

TEACHERS SHOULD
BE THE HIGHEST
PAID EMPLOYEES
ON EARTH.

Anonymous

**ONCE YOU HAVE LEARNED HOW TO ASK QUESTIONS – RELEVANT AND APPROPRIATE AND SUBSTANTIAL – YOU HAVE LEARNED HOW TO LEARN.**

NEIL POSTMAN AND CHARLES WEINGARTNER

I'M NOT AFRAID OF
STORMS, FOR I'M
LEARNING HOW TO
SAIL MY SHIP.

Louisa May Alcott

# WHEN YOU TEACH YOUR SON, YOU TEACH YOUR SON'S SON.

THE TALMUD

# TEACHERS
## WHO INSPIRE
REALIZE THERE WILL
ALWAYS BE ROCKS IN THE
ROAD AHEAD OF US. THEY
WILL BE STUMBLING BLOCKS
OR STEPPING STONES; IT
ALL DEPENDS ON HOW
WE USE THEM.

ANONYMOUS

YOU SEEM TO

ALWAYS

KNOW THE

ANSWER

A TRUE TEACHER SHOULD
PENETRATE, TO WHATEVER IS
VITAL IN HIS PUPIL, AND DEVELOP
THAT BY THE LIGHT AND HEAT
OF HIS OWN INTELLIGENCE.

Edwin Percy Whipple

"

THE BEST TEACHER
IS THE ONE WHO
SUGGESTS RATHER
THAN DOGMATIZES,
AND INSPIRES HIS
LISTENER WITH
THE WISH TO
TEACH HIMSELF.

Edward Bulwer-Lytton

"

A TEACHER'S PURPOSE IS NOT TO CREATE STUDENTS IN HIS OWN IMAGE, BUT TO DEVELOP STUDENTS WHO CAN CREATE THEIR OWN IMAGE.

Anonymous

AN INVESTMENT
IN KNOWLEDGE
PAYS THE
BEST INTEREST.

BENJAMIN FRANKLIN

WHAT NOBLER EMPLOYMENT,
OR MORE VALUABLE TO THE
STATE, THAN THAT OF THE
MAN WHO INSTRUCTS THE
RISING GENERATION?

Cicero

# THE IMPORTANT THING IS NOT SO MUCH THAT EVERY CHILD SHOULD BE TAUGHT, AS THAT EVERY CHILD SHOULD BE GIVEN THE WISH TO LEARN.

JOHN LUBBOCK

THOSE WHO EDUCATE CHILDREN
WELL ARE MORE TO BE
HONOURED THAN PARENTS,
FOR THESE ONLY GAVE LIFE,
THOSE THE ART OF LIVING WELL.

Aristotle

**ONE CHILD, ONE TEACHER, ONE BOOK AND ONE PEN CAN CHANGE THE WORLD.**

Malala Yousafzai

# THE MEDIOCRE TEACHER TELLS. THE GOOD TEACHER EXPLAINS. THE SUPERIOR TEACHER DEMONSTRATES. THE GREAT TEACHER INSPIRES.

WILLIAM ARTHUR WARD

TEACHING IS
LEAVING A
VESTIGE OF
ONESELF IN THE
DEVELOPMENT
OF ANOTHER.

EUGENE P. BERTIN

WHAT OFFICE IS THERE
WHICH INVOLVES MORE
RESPONSIBILITY, WHICH
REQUIRES MORE QUALIFICATIONS,
AND WHICH OUGHT, THEREFORE,
TO BE MORE HONOURABLE
THAN THAT OF TEACHING?

**HARRIET MARTINEAU**

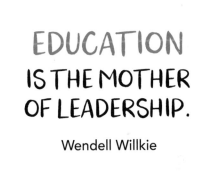

# EDUCATION
## IS THE MOTHER
## OF LEADERSHIP.

Wendell Willkie

SELDOM EVER WAS ANY
KNOWLEDGE GIVEN TO KEEP,
BUT TO IMPART: THE GRACE
OF THIS RICH JEWEL IS
LOST IN CONCEALMENT.

Joseph Hall

YOU HAVE

HELPED ME

ENJOY

SCHOOL

**IF YOU WOULD THOROUGHLY KNOW ANYTHING, TEACH IT TO OTHERS.**

Tryon Edwards

THE DREAM BEGINS WITH
A TEACHER WHO BELIEVES
IN YOU, WHO TUGS AND
PUSHES AND LEADS YOU
TO THE NEXT PLATEAU.

Dan Rather

TEACHING SHOULD BE FULL OF IDEAS INSTEAD OF STUFFED WITH FACTS.

Anonymous

# WE CANNOT HOLD A TORCH TO LIGHT ANOTHER'S PATH WITHOUT BRIGHTENING OUR OWN.

BEN SWEETLAND

SOMEWHERE, SOMETHING
INCREDIBLE IS WAITING
TO BE KNOWN.

Sharon Begley

# BY TEACHING, WE LEARN.

LATIN PROVERB

NATURAL ABILITY
IS BY FAR THE BEST,
BUT MANY MEN
HAVE SUCCEEDED
IN WINNING HIGH
RENOWN BY SKILL
THAT IS THE FRUIT
OF TEACHING.

PINDAR

IT IS THE SUPREME ART OF THE
TEACHER TO AWAKEN JOY
IN CREATIVE EXPRESSION
AND KNOWLEDGE.

Albert Einstein

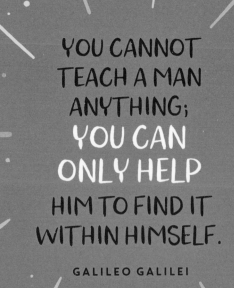

YOU CANNOT
TEACH A MAN
ANYTHING;
YOU CAN
ONLY HELP
HIM TO FIND IT
WITHIN HIMSELF.

**GALILEO GALILEI**

WHAT THE TEACHER IS
IS MORE IMPORTANT
THAN WHAT HE TEACHES.

Karl Menninger

"

ONE LOOKS BACK
WITH APPRECIATION
TO THE BRILLIANT
TEACHERS, BUT
WITH GRATITUDE
TO THOSE WHO
TOUCHED OUR
HUMAN FEELINGS.

Carl Jung

"

YOU

ARE MY

FAVOURITE

TEACHER

THE MOST EFFECTIVE TEACHER
WILL ALWAYS BE BIASED,
FOR THE CHIEF FORCE IN
TEACHING IS CONFIDENCE
AND ENTHUSIASM.

Joyce Cary

IT IS A LUXURY
TO LEARN; BUT
THE LUXURY
OF LEARNING
IS NOT TO BE
COMPARED
WITH THE
LUXURY OF
TEACHING.

ROSWELL DWIGHT HITCHCOCK

EDUCATION IS THE GUARDIAN
GENIUS OF DEMOCRACY. IT
IS THE ONLY DICTATOR THAT
FREE MEN RECOGNIZE, AND
THE ONLY RULER THAT FREE
MEN REQUIRE.

Mirabeau B. Lamar

THE WHOLE PURPOSE
OF EDUCATION IS
TO TURN MIRRORS
INTO WINDOWS.

Sydney J. Harris

# TO ME, EDUCATION IS A LEADING OUT OF WHAT IS ALREADY THERE IN THE PUPIL'S SOUL.

MURIEL SPARK

# A GOOD TEACHER

IS A MASTER OF SIMPLIFICATION AND AN ENEMY OF SIMPLISM.

LOUIS A. BERMAN

# NINE TENTHS OF EDUCATION IS ENCOURAGEMENT.

Anatole France

THE TRUE AIM
OF EVERYONE WHO
ASPIRES TO BE A
TEACHER SHOULD BE
NOT TO IMPART HIS
OWN OPINIONS, BUT
TO KINDLE MINDS.

FREDERICK WILLIAM
ROBERTSON

TEACHERS WHO INSPIRE
KNOW THAT TEACHING IS
LIKE CULTIVATING A GARDEN,
AND THOSE WHO WOULD
HAVE NOTHING TO DO WITH
THORNS MUST NEVER ATTEMPT
TO GATHER FLOWERS.

Anonymous

**" "**

HE THAT TEACHES
US ANYTHING
WHICH WE KNEW
NOT BEFORE IS
UNDOUBTEDLY TO BE
REVERENCED AS
A MASTER.

Samuel Johnson

# EDUCATION IS THE MOVEMENT FROM DARKNESS TO LIGHT.

ALLAN BLOOM

THE TASK OF THE EXCELLENT
TEACHER IS TO STIMULATE
"APPARENTLY ORDINARY"
PEOPLE TO UNUSUAL EFFORT.
THE TOUGH PROBLEM IS NOT
IN IDENTIFYING WINNERS;
IT IS IN MAKING WINNERS
OUT OF ORDINARY PEOPLE.

K. Patricia Cross

YOU ARE

ALWAYS

FAIR

**IF YOU HAVE KNOWLEDGE, LET OTHERS LIGHT THEIR CANDLES WITH IT.**

Margaret Fuller

# I HEAR AND I FORGET. I SEE AND I REMEMBER. I DO AND I UNDERSTAND.

CHINESE PROVERB

BE CAREFUL TO LEAVE YOUR
SONS WELL INSTRUCTED
RATHER THAN RICH, FOR THE
HOPES OF THE INSTRUCTED
ARE BETTER THAN THE WEALTH
OF THE IGNORANT.

Epictetus

FINALLY,
EDUCATION ALONE
CAN CONDUCT US TO
THAT ENJOYMENT
WHICH IS, AT ONCE,
BEST IN QUALITY
AND INFINITE IN
QUANTITY.

HORACE MANN

I AM INDEBTED TO
MY FATHER FOR LIVING,
BUT TO MY TEACHER
FOR LIVING WELL.

Alexander the Great

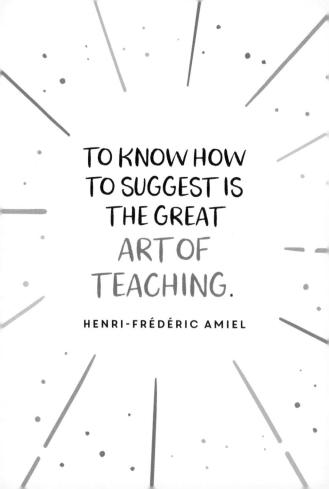

TO KNOW HOW
TO SUGGEST IS
THE GREAT
ART OF
TEACHING.

HENRI-FRÉDÉRIC AMIEL

**"**

EDUCATION IS THE
TRANSMISSION OF
CIVILIZATION... IT
HAS TO BE LEARNED
AND EARNED BY EACH
GENERATION ANEW.

Will and Ariel Durant

**"**

A SCHOOLMASTER
SHOULD HAVE AN
ATMOSPHERE OF
AWE, AND WALK
WONDERINGLY, AS
IF HE WAS AMAZED
AT BEING HIMSELF.

WALTER BAGEHOT

A MASTER CAN TELL YOU
WHAT HE EXPECTS OF YOU.
A TEACHER, THOUGH, AWAKENS
YOUR OWN EXPECTATIONS.

Patricia Neal

EDUCATION MAKES A PEOPLE
EASY TO LEAD, BUT DIFFICULT
TO DRIVE; EASY TO GOVERN,
BUT IMPOSSIBLE TO ENSLAVE.

Henry Brougham

I HAVE

LEARNED

SO MUCH

FROM YOU

"

OUR PROGRESS AS
A NATION CAN BE
NO SWIFTER THAN
OUR PROGRESS IN
EDUCATION... THE
HUMAN MIND IS OUR
FUNDAMENTAL
RESOURCE.

John F. Kennedy

EDUCATION IS SIMPLY THE SOUL OF A SOCIETY AS IT PASSES FROM ONE GENERATION TO ANOTHER.

G. K. CHESTERTON

IT IS, IN FACT, A PART OF THE FUNCTION OF EDUCATION TO HELP US ESCAPE, NOT FROM OUR OWN TIME — FOR WE ARE BOUND BY THAT — BUT FROM THE INTELLECTUAL AND EMOTIONAL LIMITATIONS OF OUR TIME.

T. S. Eliot

# INSTRUCTION ENDS IN THE SCHOOLROOM, BUT EDUCATION ENDS ONLY WITH LIFE.

FREDERICK WILLIAM ROBERTSON

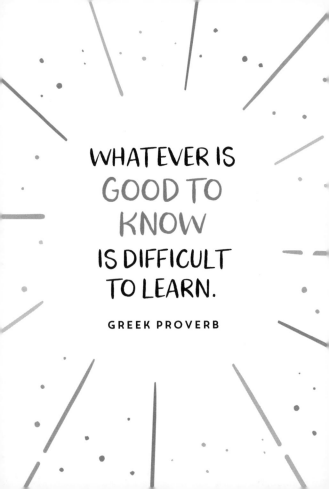

"IN TEACHING WE RELY ON THE "NATURALS", THE ONES WHO SOMEHOW KNOW HOW TO TEACH.

Peter Drucker

EDUCATION IS THE ABILITY TO
LISTEN TO ALMOST ANYTHING
WITHOUT LOSING YOUR TEMPER
OR YOUR SELF-CONFIDENCE.

Robert Frost

# WHAT WE HAVE LEARNED FROM OTHERS BECOMES OUR OWN BY REFLECTION.

Ralph Waldo Emerson

A TEACHER WHO IS
ATTEMPTING TO TEACH
WITHOUT INSPIRING THE PUPIL
WITH A DESIRE TO LEARN IS
HAMMERING COLD IRON.

Horace Mann

> **THE BEST PART OF EVERY MAN'S EDUCATION IS THAT WHICH HE GIVES TO HIMSELF.**
>
> Walter Scott

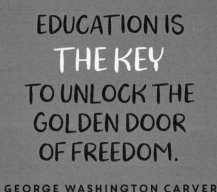

EDUCATION IS
THE KEY
TO UNLOCK THE
GOLDEN DOOR
OF FREEDOM.

GEORGE WASHINGTON CARVER

EDUCATION IS THE
APPRENTICESHIP
OF LIFE.

Robert Aris Willmott

YOU TEACH ME

TO BE A BETTER

PERSON, NOT

JUST A BETTER

STUDENT

WE THINK IT A
GREATER WORK TO
EDUCATE A CHILD,
IN THE TRUE AND
LARGE SENSE OF
THAT PHRASE, THAN
TO RULE A STATE.

WILLIAM ELLERY CHANNING

EDUCATION
IS MORE THAN
A LUXURY; IT IS A
RESPONSIBILITY
THAT SOCIETY
OWES TO ITSELF.

ROBIN COOK

THAT IS THE ONLY THING
WHICH THE MIND CAN NEVER
EXHAUST, NEVER ALIENATE,
NEVER BE TORTURED BY, NEVER
FEAR OR DISTRUST, AND
NEVER DREAM OF REGRETTING.

T. H. White on education

# A GOOD TEACHER

IS LIKE A CANDLE —
IT CONSUMES ITSELF
TO LIGHT THE WAY
FOR OTHERS.

**ANONYMOUS**

THE TRUE TEACHER DEFENDS
HIS PUPILS AGAINST HIS
OWN PERSONAL INFLUENCE...
HE GUIDES THEIR EYES FROM
HIMSELF TO THE SPIRIT THAT
QUICKENS HIM. HE WILL
HAVE NO DISCIPLES.

Amos Bronson Alcott

I BELIEVE THAT EDUCATION
IS ALL ABOUT BEING
EXCITED ABOUT SOMETHING.
SEEING PASSION AND
ENTHUSIASM HELPS PUSH
AN EDUCATIONAL MESSAGE.

Steve Irwin

# "

## TEACHING CREATES ALL OTHER PROFESSIONS.

Anonymous

"

# EDUCATION IS FOR IMPROVING THE LIVES OF OTHERS AND FOR LEAVING YOUR COMMUNITY AND WORLD BETTER THAN YOU FOUND IT.

MARIAN WRIGHT EDELMAN

"

THE ULTIMATE GOAL OF THE EDUCATIONAL SYSTEM IS TO SHIFT TO THE INDIVIDUAL THE BURDEN OF PURSUING HIS OWN EDUCATION.

John W. Gardner

# EMERALDS AS WELL AS GLASS WILL SHINE WHEN THE LIGHT IS SHED ON THEM.

JAPANESE PROVERB

NEXT IN IMPORTANCE TO
FREEDOM AND JUSTICE IS
POPULAR EDUCATION, WITHOUT
WHICH NEITHER FREEDOM
NOR JUSTICE CAN BE
PERMANENTLY MAINTAINED.

James A. Garfield

# REAL EDUCATION

SHOULD CONSIST OF DRAWING THE GOODNESS AND THE BEST OUT OF OUR OWN STUDENTS.

CESAR CHAVEZ

YOU HELP

ME SEE MY
STRENGTHS

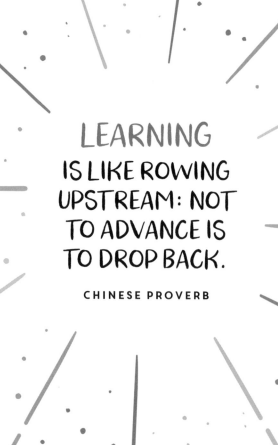

LEARNING
IS LIKE ROWING
UPSTREAM: NOT
TO ADVANCE IS
TO DROP BACK.

CHINESE PROVERB

EDUCATION'S PURPOSE:
TO REPLACE AN EMPTY MIND
WITH AN OPEN ONE.

Malcolm Forbes

**THERE ARE THREE GOOD REASONS TO BE A TEACHER — JUNE, JULY AND AUGUST.**

Anonymous

# EDUCATION MUST NOT SIMPLY TEACH WORK – IT MUST TEACH LIFE.

W. E. B. Du Bois

EDUCATION SHOULD CONSIST OF... RAISING THE INDIVIDUAL TO A HIGHER LEVEL OF AWARENESS, UNDERSTANDING AND KINSHIP WITH ALL LIVING THINGS.

Anonymous

# EDUCATION IS THE BEST PROVISION FOR OLD AGE.

ARISTOTLE

IF A DOCTOR, LAWYER OR
DENTIST HAD 40 PEOPLE IN
HIS OFFICE AT ONE TIME...
THEN HE MIGHT HAVE
SOME CONCEPTION OF THE
CLASSROOM TEACHER'S JOB.

Donald D. Quinn

THE JOB OF AN
EDUCATOR IS TO
TEACH STUDENTS
TO SEE THE VITALITY
IN THEMSELVES.

Joseph Campbell

# THERE ARE TWO KINDS OF TEACHERS: THE KIND THAT FILLS YOU WITH SO MUCH QUAIL SHOT THAT YOU CAN'T MOVE, AND THE KIND THAT JUST GIVES YOU A LITTLE PROD AND YOU JUMP TO THE SKIES.

ROBERT FROST

THE GREATEST
SIGN OF SUCCESS
FOR A TEACHER IS TO
BE ABLE TO SAY, "THE
CHILDREN ARE NOW
WORKING AS IF I
DID NOT EXIST."

MARIA MONTESSORI

EDUCATION IS NOT TO TEACH
MEN FACTS, THEORIES,
OR LAWS... BUT TO THINK
ALWAYS FOR THEMSELVES.

Robert Maynard Hutchins

GOOD
TEACHERS
MAKE THE BEST OF
A PUPIL'S MEANS;
GREAT
TEACHERS
FORESEE A
PUPIL'S ENDS.

MARIA CALLAS

YOU ARE

ALWAYS SO

ENCOURAGING

TEACHING KIDS TO COUNT IS
FINE, BUT TEACHING THEM
WHAT COUNTS IS BEST.

Bob Talbert

A TEACHER'S JOB IS TO TAKE A BUNCH OF LIVE WIRES AND SEE THAT THEY ARE WELL-GROUNDED.

Anonymous

DO NOT TRAIN A CHILD
TO LEARN BY FORCE OR
HARSHNESS; BUT DIRECT
THEM TO IT BY WHAT
AMUSES THEIR MINDS.

Plato

"

IF HE IS INDEED WISE
HE DOES NOT BID YOU
TO ENTER THE HOUSE
OF HIS WISDOM, BUT
RATHER LEADS YOU
TO THE THRESHOLD
OF YOUR OWN MIND.

**Kahlil Gibran**

# WHAT A TEACHER WRITES ON THE BLACKBOARD OF LIFE CAN NEVER BE ERASED.

ANONYMOUS

WHEN WE TAKE PEOPLE MERELY AS
THEY ARE, WE MAKE THEM WORSE;
WHEN WE TREAT THEM AS IF THEY
WERE WHAT THEY SHOULD BE, WE
IMPROVE THEM AS FAR AS
THEY CAN BE IMPROVED.

Johann Wolfgang von Goethe

# THEY MAY FORGET WHAT YOU SAID – BUT THEY WILL NEVER FORGET HOW YOU MADE THEM FEEL.

CARL W. BUEHNER

If you're interested in finding out more about our books, find us on Facebook at **Summersdale Publishers** and follow us on Twitter at **@Summersdale**.

**www.summersdale.com**